World of Whales

Beluga Whales

by Katie Chanez

Bullfrog Books

Ideas for Parents and Teachers

Bullfrog Books let children practice reading informational text at the earliest reading levels. Repetition, familiar words, and photo labels support early readers.

Before Reading
- Discuss the cover photo. What does it tell them?
- Look at the picture glossary together. Read and discuss the words.

Read the Book
- "Walk" through the book and look at the photos. Let the child ask questions. Point out the photo labels.
- Read the book to the child, or have him or her read independently.

After Reading
- Prompt the child to think more. Ask: Beluga whales make clicking noises to hunt fish. What other ways do animals hunt?

Bullfrog Books are published by Jump!
5357 Penn Avenue South
Minneapolis, MN 55419
www.jumplibrary.com

Copyright © 2024 Jump! International copyright reserved in all countries. No part of this book may be reproduced in any form without written permission from the publisher.

Library of Congress Cataloging-in-Publication Data

Names: Chanez, Katie, author.
Title: Beluga whales / by Katie Chanez.
Description: Minneapolis, MN: Jump!, Inc., [2024]
Series: World of whales | Includes index.
Audience: Ages 5–8
Identifiers: LCCN 2022051256 (print)
LCCN 2022051257 (ebook)
ISBN 9798885245869 (hardcover)
ISBN 9798885245876 (paperback)
ISBN 9798885245883 (ebook)
Subjects: LCSH: White whale—Juvenile literature.
Classification: LCC QL737.C433 C43 2024 (print)
LCC QL737.C433 (ebook)
DDC 599.5/42—dc23/eng/20221021
LC record available at https://lccn.loc.gov/2022051256
LC ebook record available at https://lccn.loc.gov/2022051257

Editor: Eliza Leahy
Designer: Emma Almgren-Bersie

Photo Credits: schankz/Shutterstock, cover; Luna Vandoorne/Shutterstock, 1; Andrea Izzotti/Shutterstock, 3; Jon Helgason/Dreamstime, 4; Capricornis/Dreamstime, 5; Chara Lupus/Shutterstock, 6–7; WaterFrame/Alamy, 8–9, 23tm; B._.B/Shutterstock, 10, 23tl; Jennifer Mackenzie/Alamy, 11, 23br; Andrey Nekrasov/Alamy, 12–13, 16–17; everst/Shutterstock, 14; Marco De Luca/Shutterstock, 15, 23bl; NOAA/NMFS/National Marine Mammal Laboratory, 18–19, 23bm; Miles Away Photography/Shutterstock, 20–21, 23tr; Christopher Meder/Shutterstock, 24.

Printed in the United States of America at Corporate Graphics in North Mankato, Minnesota.

Table of Contents

White Whale	4
Parts of a Beluga Whale	22
Picture Glossary	23
Index	24
To Learn More	24

White Whale

Look!

A white tail pops out of the water.

It belongs to a beluga whale!
This whale is white.

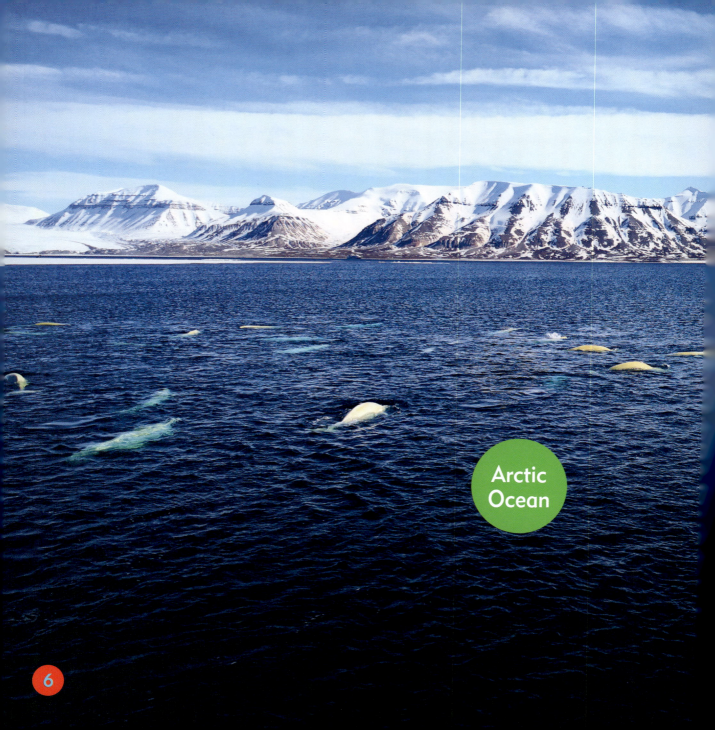

Belugas live in the Arctic Ocean.

The water is cold.

Blubber keeps the whales warm.

Fins help them swim.

They swim under ice.

A whale breathes air.
It uses its blowhole.

blowhole

It sprays water!

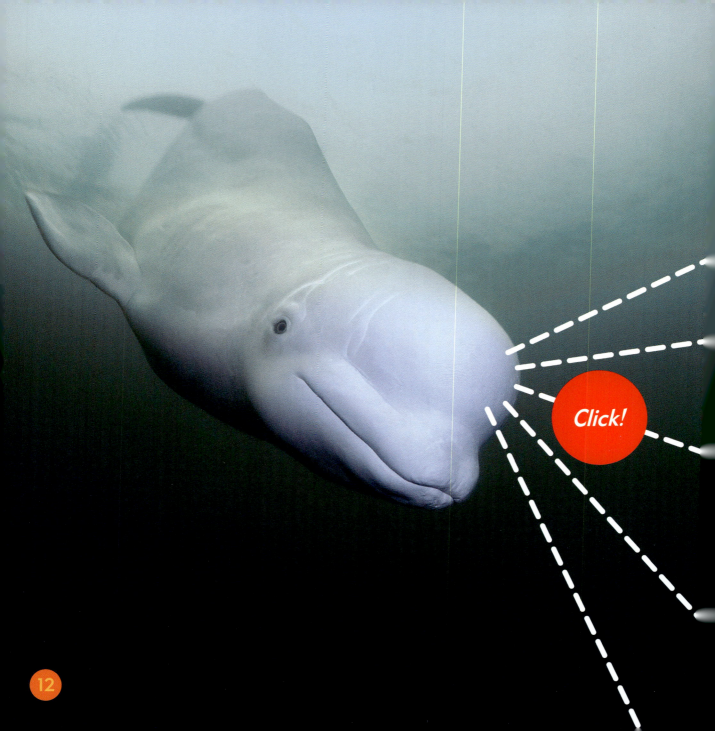

It hunts.

How?

It pushes air through its head.

This makes clicks.

The noises bounce off fish.

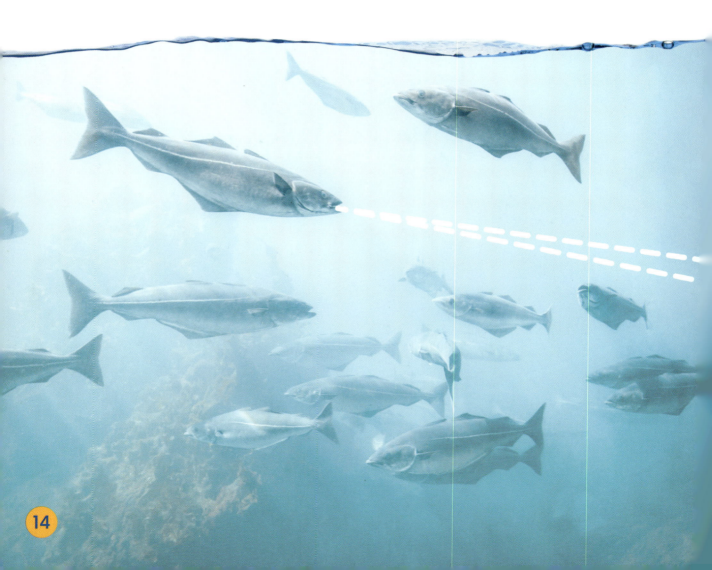

They travel to the whale's melon.

The whale learns where fish are!

melon

It tries to grabs one.
It uses its teeth.

The whale lives in a pod.
The pod swims south.
Why?
The water has less ice.

Moms have calves.
The calves grow up.
They live in the pod.

Parts of a Beluga Whale

Beluga whales can be up to 20 feet (6.1 meters) long. That is about half the length of a school bus! Take a look at the parts of a beluga whale.

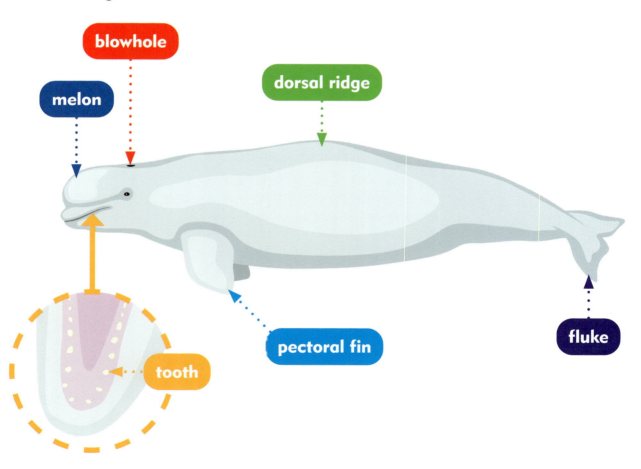

Picture Glossary

blowhole
A nostril on top of a whale's or dolphin's head used for breathing.

blubber
The layer of fat under the skin of a whale or other marine mammal.

calves
Young whales.

melon
The fatty part of a beluga's head that helps make and receive sounds.

pod
A group of whales.

sprays
Scatters liquid as drops or mist.

Index

Arctic Ocean 7
blowhole 10
calves 21
clicks 13
fins 8
hunts 13
ice 8, 18
melon 15
pod 18, 21
swim 8, 18
tail 4
teeth 17

To Learn More

Finding more information is as easy as 1, 2, 3.

❶ Go to www.factsurfer.com
❷ Enter "belugawhales" into the search box.
❸ Choose your book to see a list of websites.